BOOKS BY STEPHEN DOBYNS

POEMS

The Balthus Poems (*1982*)

Heat Death (*1980*)

Griffon (*1976*)

Concurring Beasts (*1972*)

NOVELS

Saratoga Swimmer (*1981*)

Saratoga Longshot (*1976*)

A Man of Little Evils (*1973*)

The Balthus *Poems*

STEPHEN DOBYNS

The Balthus *Poems*

ATHENEUM *New York* 1982

Acknowledgements are due to the editors of the following publications for
permission to reprint poems in this book.

Antaeus: "Farmyard at Chassy," "Landscape with Oxen," "The White
Skirt."

The Black Warrior Review: "Gottéron Landscape," "The Room."

Kayak: "The Card Game," "Dream," "The Turkish Room."

The Maine Times: "The Fortune Teller."

The Missouri Review: "Boy with Pigeons."

The New Yorker: "Getting Up," "The Window."

The North American Review: "Japanese Girl with Red Table."

Pequod: "The Children," "Larchmont," "The Moth," "Nude in Profile,"
"Nude Resting."

Poetry: "The Cherry Tree," "Girl in White," "The Golden Days," "The
Greedy Child," "The Guitar Lesson," "Katia Reading," "Landscape at
Champrovent," "The Mountain," "Patience," "The Room," "The
Street," "The Triangular Field."

I would also like to thank Michael Ryan and Rebecca Weiner for suggestions
they made about these poems, and the Corporation of Yaddo which granted
me time to complete the manuscript.

Library of Congress Cataloging in Publication Data

Dobyns, Stephen, 1941–
    The Balthus poems.

    I. Title.
PS3554.02B3   1982   811'.54   81–70061
ISBN 0–689–11278–5
ISBN 0–689–11279–3 (pbk.)

FOR JOSE BERRUEZO

"No painting can tell a story, for none can render passing time. Painting confronts us with definitive, unchanging, motionless realities. There is no picture, not even excepting those whose subject is real or supernatural events or those which give us the impression or sensation of movement, no picture in which anything happens. *In a picture things are, they do not happen."*

OCTAVIO PAZ, *discussing a painting by* BALTHUS (*Count Balthazar Klossowski de Rola*) .

The following thirty-two poems, each of which takes its title from a painting by Balthus, do not attempt to disprove the above statement. Even though they all have their beginnings in one or more of Balthus's paintings, they are not intended to interpret the paintings or explain the intentions of the artist. Rather, I tried to turn each painting into a personal metaphor to create narrative poems seemingly free from the lyrical first person voice. This is not to dismiss their debt to Balthus, which is immeasurable, but my desire was to write poems that in no way would be dependent on a knowledge of the paintings or the artist.

CONTENTS

The Balthus *Poems*

THE STREET

Across the street, the carpenter carries a golden
board across one shoulder, much as he bears the burdens
of his life. Dressed in white, his only weakness is
temptation. Now he builds another wall to screen him.

The little girl pursues her bad red ball, hits it once
with her blue racket, hits it once again. She must
teach it the rules balls must follow and it turns her
quite wild to see how it leers at her, then winks.

The oriental couple wants always to dance like this:
swirling across a crowded street, while he grips
her waist and she slides to one knee and music rises
from cobblestones—some days Ravel, some days Bizet.

The departing postulant is singing to herself. She
has seen the world's salvation asleep in a cradle,
hanging in a tree. The girl's song makes
the sunlight, makes the breeze that rocks the cradle.

The baker's had half a thought. Now he stands like a pillar
awaiting another. He sees white flour falling like snow,
covering people who first try to walk, then crawl,
then become rounded shapes: so many loaves of bread.

The baby carried off by his heartless mother is very old and
for years has starred in silent films. He tries to explain
he was accidentally exchanged for a baby on a bus, but he can
find no words as once more he is borne home to his awful bath.

First the visionary workman conjures a great hall, then
he puts himself on the stage, explaining, explaining:
where the sun goes at night, where flies go in winter, while
attentive crowds of dogs and cats listen in quiet heaps.

Unaware of one another, these nine people circle around
each other on a narrow city street. Each concentrates
so intently on the few steps before him, that not one
can see his neighbor turning in exactly different,

yet exactly similar circles around them : identical lives
begun alone, spent alone, ending alone—as separate
as points of light in a night sky, as separate as stars
and all that immense black space between them.

THE GREEDY CHILD

Gripping the mantle with thick fingers,
the maid's greedy baby reaches for fruit
in the glass and silver bowl. The baby
violently wants to become the fruit, to absorb
the fruit into his fat, transparent body.
A glass of white wine stands next to the bowl,
while nearby the nearly full bottle is reflected
in a baroque mirror with an ornate gilt frame.
But the baby has no interest in the aesthetics
of his surroundings. Instead he thrusts his hand
toward the fruit as if the bowl itself might
feel his desire and slide across the white marble,
allow the baby to suck it in, bowl and all.
Then he would tumble back, a round white heap,
and with puckered lips he would try sucking
the room toward him: he sucks and sucks until
bits of paper begin fluttering through the air,
until a gray hat rolls across the carpet, then
a pair of felt slippers, until table and chairs
crash to the floor, begin also to creep toward him;
then the Persian carpet pops its tacks and
the whole house finds itself being sucked inward,
until even people passing on the street feel a tug
as if a hand were tugging them toward the seemingly
innocuous street door of the house already half
devoured by the greedy baby in the way a worm can
devour a pear from the inside, while the baby
sits on a floor as gleaming and polished as a plate
licked clean, and he bangs his little fists
and purses his lips, and sucks and sucks,
wants to suck in all the rich and tasty world.

THE CARD GAME

The boy has never known her not to cheat,
and kneeling on the chair, leaning on the table
as if preparing to pounce, the boy is preparing
to tell her. She holds out the winning card
and he almost refuses to look at it, keeping
his head turned from her. He knows she knows
he has seen her cheating, knows she doesn't care.
He knows she thinks that were he to accuse her
he would become so angry he'd tear up the cards,
knock over the table and chairs. He might even
hit her, but instead he looks sullen and turns
half away, while she cheats and he wishes he could
break her the way he used to break her toys.
Around them, the tall green hedge seems to press
down upon them, while in the city beyond the hedge
their neighbors rob and despise each other, and in
the city beneath them rats scurry through pipes
squeaking and leaping at each other, biting and
bullying one another. At last the boy reaches to
accept the card, allows himself to be beaten as she
already knows he will do. And what has she won?
What will she take from this brother she loves?
She will place his moon face in the sky to watch
over her, keep his cat body nearby to protect her.

THE LIVING ROOM

Sunday, mid-afternoon, radiator pipes knocking
and the air thick with dry heat. Propped on one elbow,
a girl leafs through a book of photographs lying
on the yellow rug before her. She is bored and, kneeling,
she resembles a cat edging its way through tall grass.
Behind her is the piano she has just stopped playing,
practising the waltz she has spent the day learning:
the waltz her mother sometimes plays, and with which
she will surprise her parents when they return home.
On the green couch, her blond sister half sleeps,
arm out-stretched along the curved mahogany back.
In the near silent room, the girl on the couch still
hears the waltz her sister has practised over and over,
but now it seems the music comes from the orchard where
all morning she helped gather apples. With eyes shut,
she sees the orchard on the side of the hill with
the swirls and flourishes of the waltz like warm wind
between evenly spaced trees. There too among the trees
she sees her parents together, but younger and happier
than she has known them: her parents as she has seen them
in old photographs, before sickness and war and the deaths
of their own parents—her mother in a long red coat,
her father wearing a crushed felt hat lost years ago—
walking with their heads inclined toward one another,
almost touching as they talk quietly. The girl wants
to call to them, make some sign, then she realizes
that from her own body comes the sound of the waltz,
but now almost langorous, almost sad as the man and woman
ascend the hill through the orchard: Cortland, Macoun, Rose
of Caldaro, Autumnal Gray Rennet, Baldwin, Abundance—
and her parents' thin shapes among heavily laden trees.

She has always hated sunlight, and now as the dwarf,
her mother, pulls aside the curtain, allowing
the sharp triangle of light to strike her, the girl
on the day bed believes she will die, naked,
lying as she remembers Marat lay dead in his tub:
arm thrown out, chin thrust back, life flung away.
The sun pushes down on the dwarf woman's head,
forcing her down even further into her stumpy body.
Through half-closed eyes, the girl sees her mother
is dressed to look like Napoleon at the beginning
of the Egyptian campaign, but she refuses to be enticed.
After all, she is already dead. Why shouldn't she be dead,
the girl asks herself, what was there left to do?
Why couldn't she have been born the cat companion
of her own gray cat with its queer delight in death?
What secrets they could have explored together, although
even by herself the girl finds death worthy of study
and she considers being stabbed by Charlotte Corday,
her body becoming cold and stiff. But then she feels
the light from the window pressing its warmth against
her white belly and thighs, and she wonders how she can
tolerate this clumsy intrusion of the physical world?
In a moment, she will give it up, jump from bed. Today,
instead, she will explore the mysteries of language.
What book has the cat been reading? How long has her
poor mother been deaf and dumb? Lifting her pet Napoleon
in smooth cool arms, she will swirl her around the room.
Think of pyramids, think of the Sphinx, think of her own
little corporal drifting down the Nile, singing as she
will shortly sing: Oh my Rosetta, my sweet Rosetta stone.

NUDE RESTING

The girl sleeps in the small chair, her white
shirt open to expose her plump body. Only

a few minutes before, she was rushing ahead,
pursuing what she expects to be a tremendous

destiny, and shortly, when she wakes, she will again
rush forward, but here in sleep she belongs simply

to the present as she leans back, her body loosely
forming the figure "5" in the violet armchair.

In her dream, she stands to one side of a wheat field
which the setting sun has turned orange, searching

for her dog who is hidden in the wheat, invisible
except for a dark ripple that races in S-curves

over the tops of the curled heads of grain. Then,
across the field, she sees a girl waving to her,

calling something she cannot hear. The girl wears
her own yellow summer dress, and soon she realizes

it is herself waving, urgently trying to attract
her attention, while the rushing dark ripple

of her pet cocker spaniel circles and circles,
unable to discover its way out of the field.

In a moment, when the girl wakes, she will jump
to her feet, hurry from the room. She will think

there is someone who needs her and, briefly, she
will stop in the doorway, recalling a girl bathed

in orange light: a girl with something vital to
tell her, someone to provide the answers in her life.

Then she will call to her foolish dog, not sure why,
and rush to her closet to put on her yellow dress.

GETTING UP

The cat with yellow eyes doesn't yet realize
the bird is made from paper and wood. Hesitating
at the edge of its basket on the bed, the cat
stares at the toy bluebird in the girl's hand.
The girl wants to know what it's like to kill,
wants to see the cat embarrass itself, then start
washing itself. She leans back on white pillows,
white sheets, one foot just touching the floor.
She is naked and holds the bird in her right hand;
with her left she coaxes the cat, encouraging it
to leap as she watches intently with narrowed eyes.

Around her, she hears the house stirring with
morning activity: a smell of coffee from the kitchen,
a door slamming and her father's feet on the stairs.
Soon she must get up, dress for school in her
blue skirt, white blouse. Her father will drive her
on his way to work, while she finishes a report
on Argentina and its exports. Once at school,
she will join her friends, all dressed as she is,
and together they will proceed through the civilized
unwinding of their day. But now, naked with her cat,
she is learning about death and the desire
to kill; she is learning about humiliation and
the manipulation of power; and it's as if
the entire day ahead were a great inverted
pyramid resting on its tip upon these few seconds,
as the girl waits, her lips parted in a half smile,
and the cat takes a half-step, preparing to leap.

THE CHILDREN

Rain blown afternoon at the end of vacation,
their parents away taking the dog with them,
the room thick with waiting and the children
feel buried within it. Kneeling on the floor,

the girl reads a book she has read so often
she can scarcely absorb the words on the page.
Above her, leaning on the table, her younger
brother stares at the wall where he makes up

pictures in the textures of plaster and paint,
watches the same sequence over and over, sees
himself as an adult walking down a narrow street
in a rainy city, crushed black hat drawn low

on his forehead. The boy follows as his adult self
hurries down one street after another until they
reach a small restaurant, its front window
fogged and half-obscured by beads of moisture.

Peering through it, the boy sees a table where
a group of friends are joking together. The warm
smells and comfort of the restaurant are so palpable
that the boy can almost cup them in his hands,

and he wants to urge the man to enter. But instead
he finds himself forced back as if across some
river and the series of pictures begins again
with the boy following himself through the rainy city.

The boy wishes his sister could free him from this
repetition, help him proceed to the next moment,
but she only sees the page before her, has reached
the place where the young woman and her friends

await the arrival of another person. Earlier were
love affairs and the deaths of parents. Later
is war, triumph and eventual decay. But today the girl
feels so burdened by the wet afternoon that she reads

the same page over and over, can't turn to where
the friends notice the man outside the restaurant
and hurry to welcome him as he enters laughing
and shaking the rain from his hat. The children

feel so entangled in the apparent redundancy
of the single moment they no longer believe that
soon they will hear car doors slam, hear footsteps
and their dog's frantic scratching on the screen.

Instead, the girl returns to her page, and her brother
to the black umbrellas and rain-polished cars of wet
city streets as he follows his adult self, who
at the end of the block is just turning the corner.

At first she thought to save herself
from the moth, now she seeks to save the moth
from the oil lamp. Naked, fresh from bed,
the girl reaches past the moth, blocking it
from the hot glass. Her feet are cold on the floor
and as the moth bumps against her hand
part of her is furious for what she regards
as sentimental gesture, while part wants to
save the moth more than save the world itself.

Even though she thinks herself nearly a woman
and feels certain there's nothing delicate about her,
the girl partly sees the moth as like she is:
a creature fluttering toward its own destruction;
and although in irritation she is almost ready to
crush the moth, she still tries to save it, despite
the late hour and coldness of the room. The pattern
of blue and white squares on the bedframe, orange
crosses on the quilt—these are predictable

and endless. The girl partly hopes her own life
will be like that: a comfortable, predictable
pattern. The moth seemingly enamored with its
own destruction—part of her hopes her life will
be like this: turning her life over to an adventure
that might destroy her. Poised between warm bed and
oil lamp, the girl reaches out her hand as if toward
one of the adults she may become, as the moth brushes
her fingers, stains her hand with a fine gray dust.

PATIENCE

What if she ran shouting from the house? What if she
pursued their aged terrier and bit him unmercifully?
What if she rushed to the room where her mother is reading
and vomited on the rug? She's always hated that rug.

But instead she plays solitaire as the day gets later,
laying out the cards on the green baize of the old
French table with curved legs. Her mother has begged her
not to use that table; and as the girl presses one elbow

heavily upon it and hears it creak dangerously, she hopes
it will break and drive a splinter into her breast. Then
a young doctor will rush to their house and probably
fall in love with her, and despite her age her father

will give his consent. But the mere thought of her father
makes her want to scream. How *can* he keep her waiting?
Doesn't he know she has important business to do:
a skirt to buy and two books on the great poisoners

to impress her friends? As she waits, she puts the club
jack on the queen of hearts and studying their faces
she decides they must have some greater meaning, and if
she could discover that meaning she might be freed from

this terrible waiting, learn to sit calmly like her mother.
The girl thinks of the day when she was locked from the house
and as she sat on the steps hating herself and the world
around her, she was positive her better self was sitting

at the dinner table, deferring to her parents and properly
using the silver. Since then she often pictures this creature
lurking out of sight—a prim girl with blond ringlets—
ready to take her place at the first sign of a mistake.

But today she refuses to be bullied by a better self,
today she wants to be someone who bites the dog.
Bravely, she comes to the decision she was born
an orphan and she wishes she could take her father

by the lapels and shout: Admit it, I'm not your child!
Then, as she concedes another game, she seeks out
the king of spades and, admiring his sinister aspect,
demands that he claim her as his dutiful daughter.

NUDE IN PROFILE

Breasts the size of pale blue plums—the girl
pauses in morning light, fresh from her bath,
observing herself in the mirror above the basin.
As if in modesty, she holds a yellow towel
at her waist, as if her mirror were
a stranger now attempting to watch her.
Watching herself in the mirror, she feels
like such a stranger; and as she observes
the small breasts, she no longer sees them as
curiosities of her present, but objects
of her future, and so she stares at them,
trying to guess that future. After a moment,
she smiles and steps back, raises the yellow
towel in her right hand, reaches out her left
as if for the hand of a man who will someday
ask her to dance. She nods her head slightly
and lifting her arms she begins turning
in slow circles in the sunlit bathroom,
her feet gliding over the cold tile floor.
In her mind, she hears the accordion, hears
the beckoning rise and hesitation of the dance,
and she begins to twirl and spin faster, the sun
glittering on drops of water still on her skin,
as she sways and weaves with eyes half-closed,
presses the yellow towel against her breasts:
breasts the size of pale blue plums.

Hand gripping the girl's thigh, pressed nearly upon
what her Bible calls her loins, the girl's music teacher
tries to make her sing. But she will not sing.
She will not play the piano or even the guitar.
Stretched on her back across the woman's knees,
blue skirt yanked past her navel, the girl pretends
to be asleep, while with her left hand she tugs
at the top of her teacher's gray dress, freeing
the right breast which flops out above her and so
startles the girl she nearly cries out, but she
won't cry out, won't sing, won't play the guitar.
She hates those black notes on the page: the snappy
little eighth notes, self-important whole notes.
Who says they must start at the beginning
and proceed to the end? She wishes to play only
the middles of songs, sing only the half notes—
and so she and her teacher have come to quarrel.

Now her teacher's white breast hangs above her,
as round as a whole note, and the girl knows she
could sing that note if she chose, and her teacher
would be blown away as if by a singing tornado.
The girl thinks of the songs she sings to her dog
or the sounds she makes like quacking like a duck.
Her teacher hates it when she quacks like a duck.
For that matter, the girl hates the way her teacher
takes her nice fat songs and trims them to fit
black marks on a page. So she closes her eyes
and pretends to sleep, while her teacher
pulls her hair. The girl doesn't care.
In her mind, she sketches a picture of a mountain.
Then she places herself at the top, wearing
her best blue skirt, red jacket. The girl looks
to the east where the sun is impatient to rise.

So she clears her throat and begins to quack grandly
and the sun climbs into the sky like a fat shopper
on a jerky escalator, for which she thinks her music
teacher and all the tuneless world should thank her.

Wings, wings—pigeons at the glass and light gilding
their feathers, silhouetting their bodies so both
morning light and bird shadow strike the boy staring
delightedly at pigeons come for the breadcrumbs
he has sprinkled on the ledge. Since daybreak, the boy
has been performing his morning chores and now he
tends and waters the plants on the table: caladium,
begonia, dumbcane. Soon he'll make coffee, heat
sweetrolls, carry the tray to his mistress, wait
in the doorway, whispering her name till she wakes.
Already he is wearing the foolish Templars' jacket
she supplies for him, but as he stands holding
the watering can he has almost forgotten the woman
who employs him, as he gazes at the pigeons, amazed
how a single motion of wings sends them spiraling
through the air. He thinks of the dovecote on top
of the stable, how from there he can watch the road
wind through the valley toward cities in the south.
The boy taps his foot once on the floor just to feel
the floor firmly beneath him and he thinks all he
must do is walk through the door behind him to put
sweetrolls and breakfast trays behind him forever.
He sees the world's roads covering the world like
the net with which the gardener covers his berry bushes:
one road leading to the next almost forever. Nearby
a small bell begins to ring, but the boy refuses to move.
Instead, he watches the pigeons flutter at the window,
then fly up into sunlight which turns their white
wings golden as they disappear into blue morning sky.

THE CHERRY TREE

Perched on the fifth rung of the ladder, the girl
in the blue dress stretches precariously
into the tree toward the first ripe cherries.

Beyond her, the orchard of apple and cherry
glows orange with morning light spreading down
to the thick line of chestnut and birch bordering

the stream. Then rise pastures on the first slopes
of the mountain, then the mountain itself: its pink
cliff lifted high above the girl like the palm

of a hand lifted up to break her, as she will be
broken by the future she is constantly entering;
a future that will grant her a life like any other,

with hardship she is not now capable of believing—
pain of childbirth, pain of separation and death.
But the girl stretched out to take the cherries

has few fears. If she considered it at all,
she would say she intends to seize her life
in the same way she is about to take the fruit

which she will set between her teeth and suck:
suck the juice and sweet pulp into her mouth,
spit the pits in a high arc to the ground below.

GIRL IN WHITE

The girl in white sits with her hands in her lap.
Her white dress is pulled down past her shoulders
to a few inches below her breasts. She is perhaps
fourteen. The afternoon sun enters from the right,
lighting her bare shoulder, right side of her face.
She sees nothing in the room, and one by one she
is pushing away the sounds that press down upon her:
sound of parents arguing in the kitchen,
her brothers quarreling; pushing away the violent
sounds of the street: cars honking, buses heaving
themselves through January cold. In her eyes, it is
late spring, and from her bedroom window she watches
the farmer's son leading one white cow out across
the pasture with a tall pine at its center.
The wind brings her the smell of manure and freshly
turned earth. The boy wears a brown coat. Looking back,
he raises his arm as if in greeting. Although she knows
he can't see her, the girl steps away from the window.
It is early morning and she feels her life beginning.

Now, this winter afternoon, sitting with hands folded,
she imagines a man laying one hand against her cheek.
She imagines rising to embrace him, softly at first,
then harder as the buttons of his brown coat dig
into her bare skin. Standing, she presses her wrists
against her breasts, trying to imitate the rough feel
of his hands moving across her body. From the street,
she again begins to hear cars rushing at each other,
people calling and shouting; from the kitchen, she hears
someone crying, then her father's voice raised in anger.

THE ROOM

Either it's her sister or an apparition, and she hopes
it's the latter, but expects it's her sister pretending
to be invisible, since she recognizes her sister's
red socks and slippers. Otherwise the figure is naked
except for the white towel draped over one shoulder.

Kneeling by the fireplace, the girl is torn between speaking
or continuing to read her book. If she speaks, she must deal
with her sister's petulant sense of failure, yet if she
keeps quiet she must endure her sister's boasting after
parading about in a state of false invisibility.

So, despite the red socks, the girl decides it must be
an apparition, and since she has been reading about Rome
she decides the figure is an androgynous Roman
who has arrived to address the Senate on the fate of
hermaphrodites everywhere. From her place on the rug,

the girl finds androgyny more interesting than the phony
invisibility of her sister who is a year older and on the edge
of becoming a woman. The girl hasn't decided what she
thinks of becoming a woman, but knows androgyny and
invisibility are poor second choices. What she feels,

almost without knowing it, is that her own choices
have become fewer. It seems not long before that
the world around her—animals, weather, even the people
on city streets who shove and bump one another—
that every waking hour offered endless opportunity.

But now she speculates on a future in which each year
the world resumes possession of all she has borrowed,
takes back blessings she thought were hers to keep,
until she too becomes an apparition, less than invisible,
without book or Roman Senate or young sister to amuse her.

LANDSCAPE AT CHAMPROVENT

Perhaps she can see as far as Paris, perhaps Brussels.
From the hilltop where the girl has come to watch sunset,
the summer landscape of hills and pastures is spread out
in the way her toys a few years before were spread out
on the floor of her room. Here, lying in the grass,
she tries to recover that sense of omnipotence as if
she could move a field, adjust a mountain, lift the large
white house beneath her, stick it back in its wooden box.
But as she watches the patterns of countryside unroll
toward the ocean, she knows in her bedroom she never
felt the wonder she feels on most days watching the world
around her, such as she had felt that morning crossing
the fields to the village. But then she came upon the butcher
beating his dog, kicking it for stealing scraps,
lifting it by its collar and hurling it against a wall,
and even though she had seen other dogs beaten and worse,
today she felt the world was being smashed within her
and she wanted to crawl to her bed, heap blankets over her.

Here, on this hilltop at sunset, the girl is attempting
to repair her world, but in the dark line of trees,
in the huge cities she can almost see in the distance,
the girl believes she can see animals being mistreated,
people being kicked and pushed aside, as if the golden
spaces in between were only glittering distractions
from the true business of the world. And unwillingly
she realizes the landscape stretched before her
is opposite from the landscape on the floor of her room:
these fields don't belong to a world of her imagination,
but rather she belongs to the butcher's world
for it to play with her as it chooses. Watching the sun
disappear beyond the farthest hills, the girl dreads
the darkness hidden within houses, tucked beneath trees;

and as she enters the evening she feels the darkness
will never entirely pass by, as behind her from the east
she can see night approaching and with it the sound
of yelping, the sound of the butcher beating his dog.

THE MOUNTAIN

Who does the mountain belong to anyway? As Wordsworth
believed all mountains belonged to him, so these
seven people think it belongs to each of them alone.

To the left, a young man with pipe and backpack
kneels and sticks his staff hard against the rock
like a sword to a Saracen neck. In kneeling,

he copies the contours of the pinnacle behind him,
and he's of the opinion this constitutes possession.
But beside him the beautiful blond girl disagrees

as she lifts her joined hands into sunlight, mimicking
the masculine shapes of jutting rock, believing
such sympathy makes her mistress of all she surveys.

On the ground at right, a girl in a red coat pretends
to sleep, her body imitating the gentle slope, while
with her ear to the earth she hears a faint whispering

promising to love her alone. Behind her a young man
recites poetry to the stone out-cropping he would
like to become. What kind of poetry? Take a guess:

Peruvian or Swiss. A little further an old couple dawdles
at the cliff's edge. The man points to where his trucks
will remove the mountain, as his wife holds her straw hat

and nods. They plan to rebuild all this in the backyard
of their suburban home, unaware the mountain is rebuilding
them into the slight hill rising to the cliff beyond them.

Who does the mountain belong to? Rather, to whom do these
seven people belong? Only the seventh will soon
formulate an answer, as far to the right he climbs steadily

faster—a small figure in a white shirt, black vest.
He's happy to be alone, tells himself he hates people
and hopes someday to become as misanthropic as rock—

even though he desires the blond girl thrusting herself
upward in mannish postures. But he wants to think it's like
desiring himself: like walking to the top of the mountain

is like walking to the top of himself. As he climbs,
he digs his heels firmly into the rock, and feels
the pain the mountain must feel as if it were his pain.

Briefly, he looks back toward the others, to the girl
lifting her arms into blue sky—his mountain, his sky—
and he tries to see them all as fragments of himself,

see them as images of his own imagination, and he comes
to the decision there never was a mountain, that he is
sitting in his small room in the city, watching the wall

across the alley; and everyday he grows more afraid of how
alone he is, yet he refuses to ask anything of anyone:
that like a mountain he will ask nothing of all the world.

The face in the mirror is full of desire,
and the girl holding the small hand mirror
wishes the face were an elaborate creation of
golden meringue that she might nibble it slowly.
The white handle of the mirror presses
against her belly, seems to protrude from it
like the white handle of a knife, and the girl
plays with it as she leans back on the green couch—
her short skirt hitched up to thighs
turned golden in the light of the fire.
The girl feels such tenderness for the girl
in the mirror that the rest of the room
becomes as insubstantial as a room made
from spun sugar : brown table, rug, the mantle
and fire—even the boy tending the fire,
whom she has invited here and with whom she intends
to amuse herself. As for the boy, as he leans
into the fire, he likes how the extreme heat
makes his skin feel sharp and pointed.
On either side of him, the andirons have
the contemptuous expression of the sphinx.
The boy is frightened to look at the girl,
is frightened of the flat round face,
the precisely plucked eyebrows. He thinks of
the autumn night outside, of the birch
and thick maple which surround the house.
He thinks of stealing between trees so quietly
that not even the birds wake from their nervous
and fitful sleep. As he gazes into the fire,
he recalls the girl's golden skin, her small
golden dress, and he wishes he could bite
as the fire bites and devours its sticks.
What does he know of rooms like this one?
He wishes it were a forest pond that he might
snatch up and eat the golden trout at its center.

Whistle from the street, feet on the stairs—soon
her lover will come and the oriental girl leans back
on her bed, watching herself in the hand mirror,
trying to determine what he will see. Her pink robe
hangs loosely from her naked body, black hair
held back from her moon face by a white ribbon.
As she studies herself, her eyes flicker
impatiently over her body in a way she imagines
he will touch her, moving his thick white hands
upward along her thighs, upward along her soft,
pink belly to her breasts, circling and pinching
the nipples briefly between thumb and finger, then
raising his hands to encircle her neck, fingers
massaging the nape, hands so strong they could
twist her head from her; but then releasing her,
letting his fingers trail off through black hair.
Around her, the riot of blue and yellow tiles
on the wall, red tiles on the floor, clash of
orange and peach of the bed clothes—the violence
of color mimics the very violence of her lover
when at last he pushes the door open and takes her
without word or greeting: and her mouth forms
the slightest of smiles as she sees herself thrown back
on the violent bed, sees the rough masculine hands
thrust themselves toward her out of the hand mirror.

DREAM

She dreams her girl lover steals toward her
with one red poppy: red the color of her single
exposed nipple, color of her two red slippers.
She lies back on the blue couch, one slipper
just touching the carpet, head on the red cushion
behind her, green blouse open to the waist.
She dreams her lover approaches with one poppy
raised above her sleeping figure. In a moment,
the girl will bend and brush the petals
over her exposed breast, brush the flower
over her cheek until she wakes, startled;
until she sees the blond hair, the angular
tender face above her. Slowly, she will stand and
cup her lover's breasts in her hands, lower
her own red mouth to the girl's neck and bite,
fastening her teeth in the soft white flesh,
feeling the girl arch her back as the pain
cuts through her. Then she will release her,
drawing her mouth free of the delicate flesh,
resting her forehead on the flower-shaped mark.
The two will stand with their arms loosely
supporting each other in the golden room, swaying
like poplars in the first breeze of morning;
while from the room, from the whole house comes
no sound; from the world around them: no sound.

THE TRIANGULAR FIELD

In bright morning sunlight, the horse appears pink,
and the man is so pleased to see it that he waves
as he walks toward it across the triangular field.
The horse glances up from between two apple trees
and waits. The man was awakened early by dreams of
winter and self-doubt, dreams of no money in the bank;
and now he wants to clear his head by galloping bareback
through summer lanes with dust billowing around him,
light flickering around him in a hundred shades of green.
And he decides to gallop so fast that all the impediments
and small debts of his life will be lost in a swirl
of debris, that even his own death which he thinks
must be as gnarled as the trunks of surrounding trees
will be left deserted and despairing in the middle
of some sun-choked lane.
                        As he walks toward the horse,
he anticipates the swell of its body beneath him,
pushing out his thighs as he lies with heels pressed
against its belly, urging it to gallop even faster.
And he's sorry he can't take this back to the city:
simply, the flickering light and smell of summer grasses.
Then, in winter, when he and the world fought one another
and he gnawed at himself, was cruel to people around him,
he would think of the morning he galloped the pink horse
between apple trees, and the world fitted together
without angry words and extra pieces, and across
the lurching sky he saw his own name hastily scrawled
as if on an IOU from somebody notoriously disreputable,
someone who has never been known to tell the truth,
but who for the brief moment he has chosen to believe.

THE WHITE SKIRT

For an hour he wonders what the girl could be thinking
as she sits in the green armchair with her head
slightly lowered, her thick red hair slightly
falling forward. She has unbuttoned her white blouse
and her breasts hang loosely in the halter of her slip.

The man watches from the balcony of an apartment next door.
Strings of Christmas lights dangle between palm trees.
Through the open French windows, the man considers how
the girl stares at some spot on the floor to the right
of her red slippers, the elaborate folds of her white skirt.

Next to him, a neighbor complains that his wife and children
don't love him, while inside the man watches his own wife
dancing with their host: one fat hand massaging
the small of her back. The man would like to go home,
but senses the emptiness of his house waiting for him.

Now he notices how the girl's bare arms hang loosely
over the arms of her chair, that her whole body is limp
as if she'd been dancing all night; as if her lover
had just left her to move to another city; as if
in the knowledge of her beauty, she bears the knowledge

of her own mortality which will at last fall across
whatever she may be doing in the way a curtain can
fall across a sunlit window. The man again considers
how silent his own house must be, like the silence
inside an empty suitcase or empty suit of clothing.

Abruptly, he stands up, leaves the apartment without
speaking to his wife. He feels his life evading him,
slipping past like a puff of air between open fingers.
Once outside he seeks out the lights of the girl's window,
sees the lights of the party he has left. Down the street,

he sees the darkness of his own house. He wants to knock
at the girl's door, find the words to change their lives.
Then he pauses. For every action he can imagine taking,
he imagines reasons for not taking it; for every gain,
he imagines all the losses. He takes a few steps toward

the girl's building, then a few steps back. It's the dance
he's become best at. Gnawing and arguing at himself,
he remains standing as lights blink out in the windows
around him, until his wife finds him and without speaking
grips his arm, draws him down to his own dark home.

LANDSCAPE WITH OXEN

With a small whip tucked under his arm, the farmer
leads two great oxen dragging a dead tree trunk
across the sloping field. At the bottom of the hill,
red roofed houses surround a village square, while
past the village, rising like a stone wave, the dark
mass of Cat Mountain appears almost attentive, ready
to sweep down, driving fields, barns, houses before it.

The dead tree fell during the first autumn storm and
the farmer has spent the gray afternoon cutting it up,
stacking the wood, and now he means to saw the trunk
into rough planks. The day has turned steadily colder
and as he continues home the wind snatches and presses
against him, making him bury his chin in his collar,
keep his hands deep in the pockets of his blue coat.

Each day from the world beyond the mountain comes news
of increasing war, starvation and violent death.
The farmer has one field, one small corner of the earth,
and when something falls to disorder, he deals with it
as he can. The tree is long and T-shaped. His neighbors
will urge him to build a gallows, use the planks to
make coffins; but the farmer cares only that the tree

fell across a place where winter wheat was planted.
With the boards he will build a shelter for spring lambs
that he will fatten in summer, sell in the fall, and
of this pattern of seasonal routine he has woven a life
much in the way his wife weaves the wool into thick cloth,
into such a blue jacket as the farmer is now wearing,
which the lawless wind tries uselessly to take from him.

GOTTÉRON LANDSCAPE

The stark rock bulk of Gottéron ravine rises
into autumn sky, topped by a black row of pines
whose tips jut like sawteeth against the charcoal
gray darkness. Winding across the bottom,
like a flea on a chin, a man carries a bundle
of firewood along a path above the boulder-
interrupted stream. To someone watching from
the opposite hill, the man would be invisible
if it weren't for bare branches of aspen and
birch which appear to point toward him. Even
the rocks seem to gesture toward him as if
rock and rushing water were preparing to sweep him
from the path into the massive autumn night.
Bearing a bundle of sticks as big as his body,
the man is unaware of being particularly
heroic in pursuing the details of his life
while on the verge of being swept away by
the details of the world around him. He has never
thought of himself as one of the world's brave men.
He thinks only that he's been walking a long time,
that he's hungry and the wind bites his cheeks.
He thinks of the fire in his kitchen and the stew
his wife has promised him. As the man climbs the path
above the stream, he can almost smell the garlic
and thick gravy, see the fresh white potatoes,
as if their warmth made a kind of light or even
a length of fine silk thread he can barely grip
between cold fingers but which step by perilous step
winds him home through the rock bulk of Gottéron ravine.

KATIA READING

The book is golden with an orange spine, and the girl
reading leans back in her chair, one leg outstretched,
the other tucked up : one foot on the edge of the seat.
Because of her short red skirt and purple halter,
her bare legs and feet, you decide the room is hot,
that it's a midsummer evening. But the girl reading
has forgotten the evening, the house around her,
the city beyond her, has forgotten her small body
tucked into her chair. Instead, she is encompassed
by her book in the way one is surrounded by a sunlit
summer morning, except her head is turned slightly
to one side as if she found the page too bright.

All this is a painting you have seen often, and often
you have tried to determine what the girl is reading.
At first you thought her book was something merely
frightening : the way her head is turned from the page,
the way she has forgotten the presence of her body.
It is a long thin book, too thin for a novel ;
and you have come to think it must be poetry.
Seeing her, it makes you remember the first time
you read a poem that moved you, not even realizing
it was a poem, but feeling you saw yourself on the page ;
saw yourself with nothing to redeem you, as a creature
who wears his body like an ill-fitting suit of clothes.

Perhaps you would have laid aside your book,
but so completely was the world lifted out of
its daily banality that you kept on reading.
What had your world been until then? First you
ate something, then you bought something, then you
went bowling; a world where men passed their lives
peering under the hoods of cars. And like the girl
in the painting you must have turned your head

slightly as if from a loud noise; and you too became
like someone who has left on a journey, someone who
has become the answer to his own impossible riddle:
who condemned to his room is at last free of the room.

LARCHANT

Washed golden by morning light, the red roofed
village of Larchant clusters around its church
at the edge of Fontainebleau forest. From a hill
above it, a man who has been walking most the night
notices how the village nestles in a slight declivity
in this mass of flat land, how it seems on the verge
of being swept aside by forest and winter sky
the way a woodchip is swept aside by a river. But then,
descending, the man shakes his head in disagreement
and decides in the arrangement of fields and neat
stone houses, in the cluttered geometry of streets,
the village appears stronger than the world around it,
seems to refute the trees and ice-colored sky:
that without the village the trees would creep forward
until there was only winter wind roaring deep
in the forest and men no better than hairless things
quarreling among rocks, stealing each other's sticks.
Nearing the village, the man hears roosters crowing,
and from outlying barns the sound of cows impatient
to be milked. As he passes the first houses, he begins
to take pleasure in the feel of cobblestones underfoot.
Nearby, a grocer takes down his wooden shutters and
a boy races past with a small silver pail. The man
wants to stop and speak to them, explain that he was
walking between trees even before daylight, wants
to describe the silence of those trees, describe
the village from the hilltop, how it was bathed in
golden light. But the man feels clumsy with words
and is uncertain how to speak of what moves him.
And so he only raises his hand in greeting, before
continuing into the fields, before entering between
the first trees, allowing the forest to swallow him up.

THE FORTUNE TELLER

The girl in the orange sweater will tell your future.
Already she has laid out seven blue cards and
has begun to lift the first from the round table.
She is smiling slightly, because already she knows
what the card will be. You think you are humoring
her and have asked only if you will be happy.
But she knows you won't be happy, knows your life
won't be as simple as that, and she wonders if she
should amuse you with a story of an ocean journey.

But at that moment, you observe her hesitation
as she flips over the card, begin even to sense
her concern for you; and abruptly it doesn't matter
if the card tells of an early death by drowning
or senility making you tell the same dumb story
over and over, because no matter how awful a future
she can predict, you have hurried ahead to predict
worse for yourself: humiliating sickness and decay,
the daily degradation of a stranger wiping your ass.

Then you remember one summer as a child standing
by an open window as blue curtains flapped out
over the windy street where a funeral was passing.
Although young, you knew the box held someone's
mortal remains; and in the flapping of the drapery
you suddenly saw a face of crumpled fabric, saw
the terror of a spirit now separated from its body
lost within the flower laden box, and you turned and
fled the wind-filled room, that face of summer air.

THE WINDOW

The woman who is waiting for the evening draws
a black line over one eyebrow, then rises from
her dressing table, walks to the gramophone.

Immediately, the tremulous voice of Ada Falcon
singing "Garden of Desire" fills the room
like a perfume whose smell slides over the walls,

over the table by the window and into the autumn
afternoon, crosses the street and drifts through
the top story window of a retired clerk who sits

in his slippers at a table shuffling cards. His
wife is making cabbage soup and all day that smell
his filled his life. Now the tango draws him toward

the window where in the street he sees two children,
perhaps six or seven, poised cheek to cheek, their
joined hands thrust forward like the prow of a ship,

who remain motionless as the woman on the record
sings about loss. As he listens, the clerk recalls
dances he attended as a young man, thinks of a dance

at the seashore where he had gone with his parents.
The dance floor was a pier over the water and pines
along the shore swayed in a summer wind. Standing

at the window, the man begins to see strings of
colored lights, the band in white shirts with blue
ruffles on the sleeves. He tries to picture the faces

of the girls, but sees only a style of hair, a ribbon;
smells the mixture of perfume and sweat; sees the ocean
with white caps emerging like messages from the dark.

He assumed he would someday cross that ocean,
win for himself a life of wealth and excitement—
all the things that never happened, for his life

took other unexpected turnings: a job in an office,
illness, a childless marriage, days falling around him
like scattered cards, bringing him at last to this

small apartment on a small street where his life
seems wrapped in the smell of cabbage soup.
Looking down at the boy and girl poised motionless

in the street, the man wants to call to them.
But what could he say? Instead, he turns aside as
the children take one step, then another, hearing

only the music as their feet stumble forward,
gripping each other tightly as they spin and dip.
Look, they say, see how gracefully we are dancing.

The Japanese girl thinks she will die today.
In her mirror, she sees she is already dying
and she tries to compose her face into how
it will appear in death: forgiving, forgetful.
Between her white breasts, she already sees
the red mark of the knife—red as the red table
on the floor behind her, red as the red border
of the purple robe falling open around her
as she kneels before her mirror. Yes, she thinks,
she will destroy herself today; and her lover,
who has not come, will hear of it from people
crying to each other as he passes on the street
with his destination a solid object in his mind,
as real as the red table or the black and white
vase upon the table. He will hear that a girl
has been found with a knife in her breast,
but he won't believe it's she as he continues
toward the red table in his mind. Then at last
some friend will bring him the news, tell him
while he sits with his wife in the early evening,
eating sweets and drinking tea as he describes
the small business of his day. He will be holding
a porcelain cup with a picture of a single gull,
and he will listen to how a girl has been found
lying naked in her own blood on the golden rug
he gave her, while within him the words will be
eating his body as fire eats paper, as he tries
hopelessly to hold his cup steady and make no face.

FARMYARD AT CHASSY

From the window of your sickroom, you look out
across the farmyard to the arch of the front gate.
A man in a blue coat stands in the road. It's raining
and his reflection glimmers in the water at his feet.
To your left and right, the stone farm buildings
seem deserted, although you smell the damp smell
of hay and manure, and sometimes you hear your horse
stamp once in the barn, then fall silent. For a week,
you have lain bored and feverish, and looking out
this wet afternoon, you see no living thing except
the man in the roadway, but he stands so quietly
you begin to doubt him, wondering if he is some
trick of the eye, some accidental configuration
of branches resembling a man. But you know very well
you haven't imagined him and you begin to worry
he might demand something from you, something as
inescapable as taxation or death; and you become so
uncertain, you want to erase the very thought of him
and in your fever you decide it's you standing there,
that you are on your way to warm lands to the south,
and for a moment you have halted at this farmyard
without animals or even wet pigeons ducked beneath
rickety eaves, a farmyard so poor that you doubt
it could even keep a man alive, and you shiver
briefly, glad you don't live there, and pass on.

All this occurs at the intersection of two streets:
an old woman with a straw hat and black cane
approaches from the left, while with his back to you
a man wearing a blue sweater walks toward her.

The man is tall, erect and carries a loaf of bread.
He plans to pass through the doorway in front of him,
climb the stairs to a room where he'll eat lunch
and muse over the possibilities of his life to come.

It would strike him as inconceivable that he might
never pass the old woman. Who knows that he won't?
Not the fleecy white dog at his feet, nor the girl
with a doll, nor the young woman behind her

talking to a child in the window. Perhaps the man
with a swollen face in a doorway at far left knows
what will happen and that is why he stands back,
refuses to take part in the activity of the street.

Closest to you, standing in the street, a girl
in a yellow blouse stares directly at you, holding
her chin in her hand. She wants to see your face
when the old woman touches the man with her cane,

wants to see whether you respond with fear or
mere incomprehension, thinking it must be some joke,
as if the unfolding of the world were a story told
for your amusement alone. Only the angular man

sitting on the curb to your right seems indifferent
to what will happen. Dressed in black, he looks like
a retired juggler or acrobat. He saw the man pass
carrying a loaf of bread, and knows you are watching,

knows the man will meet his death at the intersection
in front of the printing office, that he will stop
as if struck by a sudden thought, look surprised
as if struck by a sudden memory of his childhood,

that he will drop the bread and sink to one knee.
He knows the woman at the window will call out
and the others will run to him, all except the girl
in the yellow blouse who will continue to study your face.

The angular man sees daily how people proceed through
the city with their small anticipations such as simply
eating lunch or passing through a doorway, and it seems
to him that people move in elaborate shells like

the decorated shells of eggs, that each seems to see
his immediate future as a film played on the inside
of the shell; and in the imagined fulfillment of their
desires, each thinks of the present as already gone by.

The head of the man in the blue sweater is such a shell
as he proceeds toward a future he can almost touch,
unaware of the old woman with her shiny black purse,
not noticing how she lifts her cane as he approaches.

The angular man folds himself into himself, not wanting
to watch as the old woman stretches out her cane to touch
the eggshell head which like a shell cracks and breaks,
while the girl in the yellow blouse lifts her chin and smiles.

STEPHEN DOBYNS

Stephen Dobyns was born in Orange, New Jersey, in 1941, and raised in New Jersey, Michigan, Virginia and Pennsylvania. He was educated at Shimer College, Wayne State University and The University of Iowa. He has taught at various colleges, including Boston University, The University of Iowa and The University of New Hampshire; and has worked as a reporter for The Detroit News. *His first book of poems,* Concurring Beasts, *was the Lamont Poetry Selection for 1971. His second book of poems,* Griffon, *appeared in 1976 and his third,* Heat Death, *in 1980. He has also published three novels:* A Man of Little Evils *(1973),* Saratoga Longshot *(1976) and* Saratoga Swimmer *(1981). He currently teaches in the MFA-Writing Program at Warren Wilson College and lives, with his wife and son, in Searsport, Maine.*